Books I Can Read

Paul

by
Gladys Sims Stump

Copyright © 1978 by
Southern Publishing Association
SBN 8127-0165-8

This book was
Edited by Richard W. Coffen
Designed by Mark O'Connor
Illustrated by Dean Shelton
Type set: 18/20 Spartan Medium
Printed in U.S.A.

Southern Publishing Association, Nashville, Tennessee

Jesus is God's Son.
God sent Him down here
to show people what to do.
By and by Jesus went back
to His Father.
But He left some helpers here.

Some bad men didn't like Jesus.
These bad men were not Jesus' helpers.
They talked to Saul about Jesus.
"Jesus is not good," the bad men said.
"We don't like Him."

Yes, the bad men said
bad things about Jesus.
And Saul listened.
Then he didn't like Jesus.
But Saul didn't know Jesus.

The bad men wanted
to do bad things to Jesus' helpers.
These bad men went looking
for Jesus' helpers.
Jesus' helpers were telling about
good, kind Jesus.

"You must not tell about Jesus," said the bad men.

"We will not let you tell about Jesus. We will do bad things to you if you do."

And the bad men went looking for Jesus' helpers.

"Will you help us, Saul?" the bad men asked.
"We want to find all Jesus' helpers. We will do bad things to them. We will not let one stay around. Help us, Saul."

"Yes, I will help do something with Jesus' helpers," said Saul.
"They are bad.
We will go after them."

Jesus' helpers were not bad.
They did good things.
They told all about the good Jesus.
They were kind.
They were like Jesus.

But Saul didn't know Jesus.
So he said that he
would help the bad men.
Yes, he said that he would help
the bad men who didn't like
Jesus or His helpers.

Saul went here.
Saul went there.
Saul did bad things to Jesus' helpers.
He sent them away from their homes.
Saul was bad, very bad!

"I am going to Damascus," said Saul.
"I will find all who are Jesus' helpers.
They cannot stay in their homes."
"Here, Saul," said the bad men.
"These letters will help you.
These letters tell all that
you can go after Jesus' helpers."

So Saul took the letters.
He went on his way to Damascus.
He had some helpers with him.
Saul was going to do bad things to
Jesus' helpers in Damascus.
Saul and his bad men
were on the way to Damascus.

All at once something happened.
All at once a very bright light shown all around Saul.
The light was from Jesus.
Saul was afraid.
He fell down.

Saul heard something.
It was Jesus talking.
Saul heard Jesus say,
"Saul, Saul, why are you doing what you are doing to Me and My helpers?"

Saul asked, "Who are You, Lord?"
"I am Jesus," He said.
"I am the One to whom you are doing these bad things."

Saul was surprised.
He was afraid.
"What do You want me to do?" Saul asked.
"Get up and go into the city," said Jesus.
"And you shall be told what to do."

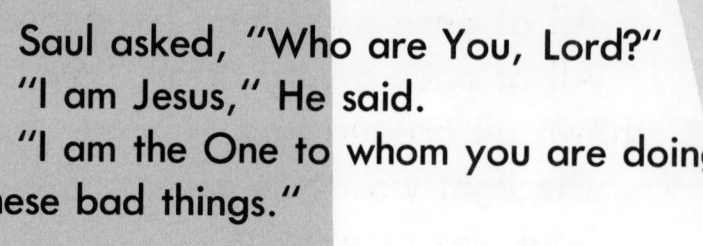

The men who were with Saul didn't see anyone, but they heard Jesus talking.
They were afraid too.

Saul got up from where he fell.
He opened his eyes.
But he couldn't see.
He was blind.
Saul had seen Jesus.
Saul had seen the bright light around Jesus.
Saul would never forget.

One of his men took Saul's hand and led him to Damascus.
But Saul didn't know what to do.
He didn't eat or drink for three days.

Saul had seen Jesus.
He would never forget.
Now Saul wanted to be one of Jesus' helpers.
He was sorry about the bad things he had done.
He was very sorry.

Jesus sent Ananias to help Saul.
Ananias was one of Jesus' helpers.
But Ananias was afraid of Saul.
"Don't be afraid of him," said Jesus.
"Saul is My man now.
He will work for Me."

Ananias did what Jesus said.
Saul could see then.

Saul said, "All must know about Jesus.
I will tell all about Jesus.
He is my Jesus now."

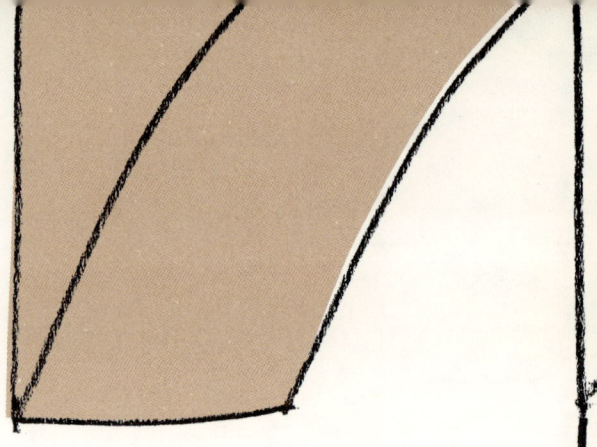

The bad men didn't
want Saul to tell about Jesus.
 They did not like Jesus.
 And now they did not like Saul.
 "You cannot tell about Jesus,"
they said.
 "We will not let you do this."

 "We will get him
and take him away," they said.
 "Let us look for him.
 We will do something bad to him.
 Yes, we will find Saul.
 We will not let Saul tell about
Jesus."

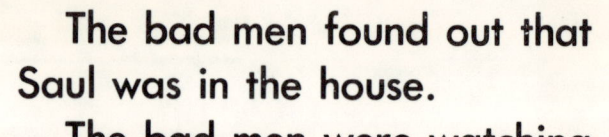

The bad men found out that Saul was in the house.
The bad men were watching by the house.
They wanted to get Saul.
But angels were with him.
They watched over him.
Jesus' helpers were there too.

"I know what we can do," said one of Jesus' helpers.

"The bad men are watching the door.

But we will put Saul in this big basket.

We will put a rope on the basket.

We will let the basket go down out of a window.

The bad men will not see.

Then Saul can get away.

He can tell about Jesus."

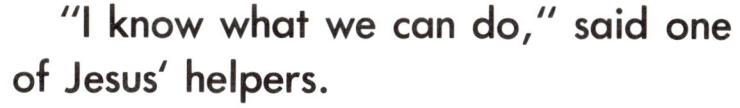

"Come here, Saul," said one of Jesus' helpers.

"See this big basket?

See the rope?

We will put you in this basket.

We will let you down from the window.

The bad men will not see.

You can get away and tell about Jesus."

"I will get into the basket," said Saul.

"I will go away and tell about Jesus."

So Saul got into the basket.

Down, down went the basket.

The bad men did not see him.

Saul's angel went with him.

Saul kept telling all about good Jesus.

His name now became Paul—not Saul.

Based on Acts 9:1-25